foundations

SMALL GROUP STUDY GUIDE

WRITTEN BY tom HOLLaDay AND kay waRReN

THE SECOND COMING

 ZONDERVAN®

SADDLEBACK CHURCH

ZONDERVAN.com/
AUTHORTRACKER
follow your favorite authors

Foundations: *The Second Coming Study Guide*
Copyright © 2003, 2004, 2008 by Tom Holladay and Kay Warren

Requests for information should be addressed to:
Zondervan, *Grand Rapids, Michigan* 49530

ISBN 978-0-310-27695-1

08 09 10 11 12 13 14 15 16 17 18 • 23 22 21 20 19 18 17 16 15 14 13 12 11 10 9 8 7 6 5 4 3 2 1

foundations TABLE OF CONTENTS

FOREWORD

What *Foundations* Will Do for You

I once built a log cabin in the Sierra Mountains of northern California. After ten backbreaking weeks of clearing forest land, all I had to show for my effort was a leveled and squared concrete foundation. I was discouraged, but my father, who built over a hundred church buildings in his lifetime, said, "Cheer up, son! Once you've laid the foundation, the most important work is behind you." I've since learned that this is a principle for all of life: you can never build *anything* larger than the foundation can handle.

The foundation of any building determines both its size and strength, and the same is true of our lives. A life built on a false or faulty foundation will never reach the height that God intends for it to reach. If you skimp on your foundation, you limit your life.

That's why this material is so vitally important. *Foundations* is the biblical basis of a purpose-driven life. You must understand these life-changing truths to enjoy God's purposes for you. This curriculum has been taught, tested, and refined over ten years with thousands of people at Saddleback Church. I've often said that *Foundations* is the most important class in our church.

Why You Need a Biblical Foundation for Life

- *It's the source of personal growth and stability.* So many of the problems in our lives are caused by faulty thinking. That's why Jesus said the truth will set us free and why Colossians 2:7a (CEV) says, *"Plant your roots in Christ and let him be the foundation for your life."*

- *It's the underpinning of a healthy family.* Proverbs 24:3 (TEV) says, *"Homes are built on the foundation of wisdom and understanding."* In a world that is constantly changing, strong families are based on God's unchanging truth.

- **It's the starting point of leadership.** You can never lead people farther than you've gone yourself. Proverbs 16:12b (MSG) says, *"Sound leadership has a moral foundation."*

- **It's the basis for your eternal reward in heaven.** Paul said, *"Whatever we build on that foundation will be tested by fire on the day of judgment . . . We will be rewarded if our building is left standing"* (1 Corinthians 3:12, 14 CEV).

- **God's truth is the only foundation that will last.** The Bible tells us that *"the sound, wholesome teachings of the Lord Jesus Christ . . . are the foundation for a godly life"* (1 Timothy 6:3 NLT), and that *"God's truth stands firm like a foundation stone . . ."* (2 Timothy 2:19 NLT).

Jesus concluded his Sermon on the Mount with a story illustrating this important truth. Two houses were built on different foundations. The house built on sand was destroyed when rain, floods, and wind swept it away. But the house built on the foundation of solid rock remained firm. He concluded, *"Therefore everyone who hears these words of mine and puts them into practice is like a wise man who built his house on the rock"* (Matthew 7:24 NIV). *The Message* paraphrase of this verse shows how important this is: *"These words I speak to you are not incidental additions to your life . . . They are foundational words, words to build a life on."*

I cannot recommend this curriculum more highly to you. It has changed our church, our staff, and thousands of lives. For too long, too many have thought of theology as something that doesn't relate to our everyday lives, but *Foundations* explodes that mold. This study makes it clear that the foundation of what we do and say in each day of our lives is what we believe. I am thrilled that this in-depth, life-changing curriculum is now being made available for everyone to use.

— Rick Warren, author of *The Purpose Driven® Life*

PREFACE

Get ready for a radical statement, a pronouncement sure to make you wonder if we've lost our grip on reality: *There is nothing more exciting than doctrine!*

Track with us for a second on this. Doctrine is the study of what God has to say. What God has to say is always the truth. The truth gives me the right perspective on myself and on the world around me. The right perspective results in decisions of faith and experiences of joy. *That* is exciting!

The objective of *Foundations* is to present the basic truths of the Christian faith in a simple, systematic, and life-changing way—in other words, to teach doctrine. The question is, why? In a world in which people's lives are filled with crying needs, why teach doctrine? Because biblical doctrine has the answer to many of those crying needs! Please don't see this as a clash between needs-oriented and doctrine-oriented teaching. The truth is we need both. We all need to learn how to deal with worry in our lives. One of the keys to dealing with worry is an understanding of the biblical doctrine of the hope of heaven. Couples need to know what the Bible says about how to have a better marriage. They also need a deeper understanding of the doctrine of the Fatherhood of God, giving the assurance of God's love upon which all healthy relationships are built. Parents need to understand the Bible's practical insights for raising kids. They also need an understanding of the sovereignty of God, a certainty of the fact that God is in control, that will carry them through the inevitable ups and downs of being a parent. Doctrinal truth meets our deepest needs.

Welcome to a study that will have a lifelong impact on the way you look at everything around you and above you and within you. Helping you develop a "Christian worldview" is our goal as the writers of this study. A Christian worldview is the ability to see everything through the filter of God's truth. The time you dedicate to this study will lay a foundation for new perspectives that will have tremendous benefits for the rest of your life. This study will help you:

- Lessen the stress in everyday life
- See the real potential for growth the Lord has given you
- Increase your sense of security in an often troubling world
- Find new tools for helping others (your friends, your family, your children) find the right perspective on life
- Fall more deeply in love with the Lord

Throughout this study you'll see four types of sidebar sections designed to help you connect with the truths God tells us about himself, ourselves, and this world.

- *A Closer Look:* We'll take time to expand on a truth or look at it from a different perspective.

- *A Fresh Word:* One aspect of doctrine that makes people nervous is the "big words." Throughout this study we'll take a fresh look at these words, words like *omnipotent* and *sovereign.*

- *Key Personal Perspective:* The truth of doctrine always has a profound impact on our lives. In this section we'll focus on that personal impact.

- *Living on Purpose:* James 1:22 (NCV) says, *"Do what God's teaching says; when you only listen and do nothing, you are fooling yourselves."* In his book, *The Purpose Driven Life,* Rick Warren identifies God's five purposes for our lives. They are worship, fellowship, discipleship, ministry, and evangelism. We will focus on one of these five purposes in each lesson, and discuss how it relates to the subject of the study. This section is very important, so please be sure to leave time for it.

Here is a brief explanation of the other features of this study guide.

Looking Ahead/Catching Up: You will open each meeting with an opportunity for everyone to check in with each other about how you are doing with the weekly assignments. Accountability is a key to success in this study!

Key Verse: Each week you will find a key verse or Scripture passage for your group to read together. If someone in the group has a different translation, ask them to read it aloud so the group can get a bigger picture of the meaning of the passage.

Video Lesson: There is a video lesson segment for the group to watch together each week. Take notes in the lesson outlines as you watch the video, and be sure to refer back to these notes during your discussion time.

Discovery Questions: Each video segment is complemented by questions for group discussion. Please don't feel pressured to discuss every single question. The material in this study is meant to be your servant, not your master, so there is no reason to rush through the answers. Give everyone ample opportunity to share their thoughts. If you don't get through all of the discovery questions, that's okay.

Prayer Direction: At the end of each session you will find suggestions for your group prayer time. Praying together is one of the greatest privileges of small group life. Please don't take it for granted.

Get ready for God to do incredible things in your life as you begin the adventure of learning more deeply about the most exciting message in the world: the truth about God!

— Tom Holladay and Kay Warren

HOW TO USE THIS VIDEO CURRICULUM

Here is a brief explanation of the features on your small group DVD. These features include a *Group Lifter,* four *Video Teaching Sessions* by Tom Holladay, and a short video, *How to Become a Follower of Jesus Christ,* by Rick Warren. Here's how they work:

The Group Lifter is a brief video introduction by Tom Holladay giving you a sense of the objectives and purpose of this *Foundations* study on the church. Watch it together as a group at the beginning of your first session.

The Video Teaching Sessions provide you with the teaching for each week of the study. Watch these features with your group. After watching the video teaching session, continue in your study by working through the discussion questions and activities in the study guide.

Nothing is more important than the decision you make to accept Jesus Christ as your Lord and Savior. You will have the option to watch a short video presentation, *How to Become a Follower of Jesus Christ,* at the end of Session Four. In this brief video segment, Rick Warren explains the importance of having Christ as the Savior of your life and how you can become part of the family of God. If everyone in your group is already a follower of Christ, or if you feel there is a better time to play this segment, continue your session by turning to the Discovery Questions in your DVD study guide. You can also select this video presentation separately on the Main Menu of the DVD for viewing at any time.

Follow these simple steps for a successful small group session:

1. Hosts: Watch the video session and write down your answers to the discussion questions in the study guide before your group arrives.

2. Group: Open your group meeting by using the "Looking Ahead" or "Catching Up" section of your lesson.

3. Group: Watch the video teaching lesson and follow along in the outlines in the study guide.

4. Group: Complete the rest of the discussion materials for each session in the study guide.

It's just that simple. Have a great study together!

1

Session One

SIGNS OF JESUS' COMING

LOOKING AHEAD

1. What do you hope to get out of this small group study?

2. What emotion do you feel when you hear people talking about the second coming of Jesus Christ? Do you feel apathy? Anticipation? Anxiety? Something else? Explain what is behind the emotion you chose.

Key Verse

Therefore, prepare your minds for action; be self-controlled; set your hope fully on the grace to be given you when Jesus Christ is revealed.

1 Peter 1:13 (NIV)

BIBLE TEACHING
Watch the video lesson now and take notes in your outline on pages 3–6.

Any study of the second coming has to come with some warning labels attached.

First Warning: Don't lose personal _____
in the midst of historical and theological _____.

HOW TO APPLY SCRIPTURE

The Application Bridge

Timeless Principles

THEN

NOW

Interpretation   Implication   Personalization

1. What did the Bible passage mean to the original hearers?
2. What is the underlying timeless principle? In a word, _____ .
3. Where or how could I practice this principle?

Second Warning: Don't lose the _____ *in the* _____ .

Third Warning: Watch out for _____ *in teaching about the second coming.*

Signs of Jesus' Coming

Signs pointing to the end

> *⁵Jesus said to them, "Watch out that no one deceives you.
> ⁶Many will come in my name, claiming, 'I am he,' and will
> deceive many. ⁷When you hear of wars and rumors of wars,
> do not be alarmed. Such things must happen, but the end is
> still to come. ⁸Nation will rise against nation, and kingdom
> against kingdom. There will be earthquakes in various places,
> and famines. These are the beginning of birth pains."*
> (Mark 13:5–8 NIV)

- False _____

- _____

- _____

- _____

These signs that point to the end will all be summed up at the end. There will be wars, leading to a great final war. There will be false christs with false signs, leading to a great final Antichrist with great false signs that fool many (2 Thessalonians 2:9; Revelation 19:20). There will be famine in various places, leading to a great worldwide famine in the end (Revelation 6:5–6).

Jesus' warning about these signs: don't be _____!

Signs preceding the end

- _____

> *"At that time many will turn away from the faith and will
> betray and hate each other."* (Matthew 24:10 NIV)

> *For the time will come when men will not put up with sound
> doctrine. Instead, to suit their own desires, they will gather
> around them a great number of teachers to say what their
> itching ears want to hear.* (2 Timothy 4:3 NIV)

- _____ of personal evil

  [1]But mark this: There will be terrible times in the last days. [2]People will be lovers of themselves, lovers of money, boastful, proud, abusive, disobedient to their parents, ungrateful, unholy, [3]without love, unforgiving, slanderous, without self-control, brutal, not lovers of the good, [4]treacherous, rash, conceited, lovers of pleasure rather than lovers of God—[5]having a form of godliness but denying its power. Have nothing to do with them. (2 Timothy 3:1–5 NIV)

- _____ will come

  First of all, you must understand that in the last days scoffers will come, scoffing and following their own evil desires. (2 Peter 3:3 NIV)

- Many _____ prophets

  "And many false prophets will appear and deceive many people." (Matthew 24:11 NIV)

Signs accompanying the end

- Signs in the sun, moon, and stars

  "Immediately after the distress of those days 'the sun will be darkened, and the moon will not give its light; the stars will fall from the sky, and the heavenly bodies will be shaken.'" (Matthew 24:29 NIV)

- Roaring of the sea; heavenly bodies shaken

  "On the earth, nations will be in anguish and perplexity at the roaring and tossing of the sea." (Luke 21:25b NIV)

- Great distress (unparalleled)

  "For then there will be great distress, unequaled from the beginning of the world until now—and never to be equaled again." (Matthew 24:21 NIV)

A CLOSER LOOK
Signs of the End Times

The most detailed descriptions of the end time events are found in the book of Revelation.

The seven seals (Final Conflict)	The seven trumpets (Final Destruction)	The seven bowls (God's Wrath Is Finished)
1. White horse: Conquest	1. Earth	1. Sores
2. Red horse: War	2. Sea	2. Sea to blood
3. Black horse: Famine	3. Rivers	3. Rivers to blood
4. Pale horse: Death	4. Lights (3 woes)	4. Fire from sun
5. Martyrs	5. Demons (locusts) into darkness	5. Beast's kingdom
6. Earthquakes	6. Angels and earthquakes (1/3 of men)	6. Euphrates River dried up (Armageddon)
7. The 7th seal is the 7 trumpets	7. The 7th trumpet is the 7 bowls	7. Earthquake (It is done!)

[10b] . . . *The heavens will disappear with a roar; the elements will be destroyed by fire, and the earth and everything in it will be laid bare.* [12] . . . *That day will bring about the destruction of the heavens by fire, and the elements will melt in the heat.*
(2 Peter 3:10b, 12 NIV)

Then I saw a new heaven and a new earth, for the first heaven and the first earth had passed away . . . (Revelation 21:1 NIV)

DISCOVERY QUESTIONS

1. What helps you to avoid: getting caught up in the curiosity surrounding the end times, getting lost in the details, being polarized by a particular point of view, or losing sight of the big picture?

2. Many Christians experience fear when they study the second coming. Why do you think that is? How can we help each other move from fear to hope?

3. Look back at the outline and review the verses under the section "Signs Preceding the End." Is there anything helpful or beneficial about knowing things will get worse before they get better? If so, what?

4. Look again at your outline and review the verses under the section "Signs Accompanying the End." Does knowing this world will not last cause a change in your attitude toward any specific material thing, human government, or institution? Does it cause you to look differently at a problem or struggle you are facing?

Did You Get It? How has this week's study helped you see beyond your current circumstances to God's overall plan for human history?

Share with Someone: Think of a person you can encourage with the truth you learned in this session. Write their name in the space below and pray for God to provide that opportunity this week.

LIVING ON PURPOSE
Discipleship

One of the great truths of the second coming is the focus on Jesus Christ. During this four-week study on the second coming, memorize these verses which describe the inevitable focus on the lordship of Jesus that will take place at the end of time.

> [5]*Your attitude should be the same as that of Christ Jesus:* [6]*Who, being in very nature God, did not consider equality with God something to be grasped,* [7]*but made himself nothing, taking the very nature of a servant, being made in human likeness.* [8]*And being found in appearance as a man, he humbled himself and became obedient to death—even death on a cross!* [9]*Therefore God exalted him to the highest place and gave him the name that is above every name,* [10]*that at the name of Jesus every knee should bow, in heaven and on earth and under the earth,* [11]*and every tongue confess that Jesus Christ is Lord, to the glory of God the Father.* (Philippians 2:5-11 NIV)

For an easier assignment, memorize only verses 9 through 11.

PRAYER DIRECTION

Take some time as a group to talk about your specific prayer requests and to pray for one another. Thank God for his promise that Jesus is coming back again to right all wrongs and dry our tears.

NOTES

2

Session two

GOD'S TIMING

CATCHING UP

1. If you told someone what you learned last week about the second coming of Jesus Christ, how did they respond?

2. What did you learn during last week's "Living on Purpose" activity? As a group, say Philippians 2:9–11 (NIV) together:

   Therefore God exalted him to the highest place and gave him the name that is above every name, that at the name of Jesus every knee should bow, in heaven and on earth and under the earth, and every tongue confess that Jesus Christ is Lord, to the glory of God the Father.

Key Verse

For you know very well that the day of the Lord will come like a thief in the night.

1 Thessalonians 5:2 (NIV)

BIBLE TEACHING
Watch the video lesson now and take notes in your outline on pages 13–17.

The Time of the Second Coming

Descriptions by Jesus

- Like a _____ (Matthew 25:1-13)

- Like the destruction of _____

  ²⁸"It was the same in the days of Lot. People were eating and drinking, buying and selling, planting and building. ²⁹But the day Lot left Sodom, fire and sulfur rained down from heaven and destroyed them all. ³⁰It will be just like this on the day the Son of Man is revealed." (Luke 17:28–30 NIV)

- Like _____

  ²⁶"When the Son of Man comes again, it will be as it was when Noah lived. ²⁷People were eating, drinking, marrying, and giving their children to be married until the day Noah entered the boat. Then the flood came and killed them all." (Luke 17:26–27 NCV)

- Like a _____ in the night

  ⁴²"Therefore keep watch, because you do not know on what day your Lord will come. ⁴³But understand this: If the owner of the house had known at what time of night the thief was coming, he would have kept watch and would not have let his house be broken into. ⁴⁴So you also must be ready, because the Son of Man will come at an hour when you do not expect him." (Matthew 24:42–44 NIV)

Facts about the timing

- The time of Jesus' return is _____.

  "Behold, I am coming soon! Blessed is he who keeps the words of the prophecy in this book." (Revelation 22:7 NIV)

- The time of Jesus' return is known only by _____.

  "No one knows about that day or hour, not even the angels in heaven, nor the Son, but only the Father." (Matthew 24:36 NIV)

  ⁶So when they met together, they asked him, "Lord, are you at this time going to restore the kingdom to Israel?" ⁷He said to them: "It is not for you to know the times or dates the Father has set by his own authority." (Acts 1:6-7 NIV)

- The time of Jesus' return is _____.

  For you know very well that the day of the Lord will come like a thief in the night. (1 Thessalonians 5:2 NIV)

  "So you also must be ready, because the Son of Man will come at an hour when you do not expect him." (Matthew 24:44 NIV)

People of the End Times

1. The Man of Lawlessness/the Beast/_____

   Don't let anyone deceive you in any way, for that day will not come until the rebellion occurs and the man of lawlessness is revealed, the man doomed to destruction.
   (2 Thessalonians 2:3 NIV)

   ⁴He will oppose and will exalt himself over everything that is called God or is worshiped, so that he sets himself up in God's temple, proclaiming himself to be God. . . . ⁹The coming of the lawless one will be in accordance with the work of Satan displayed in all kinds of counterfeit miracles, signs and wonders, ¹⁰ᵃand in every sort of evil that deceives those who are perishing. (2 Thessalonians 2:4, 9-10a NIV)

A CLOSER LOOK
Understanding the Antichrist

There will be one final Antichrist among many—the end of a long line that began after Jesus' first coming. The Beast is the final and worst Antichrist, not the only antichrist.

"For many will come in my name, claiming, 'I am the Christ,' and will deceive many." (Matthew 24:5 NIV)

[18]*Dear children, this is the last hour; and as you have heard that the antichrist is coming, even now many antichrists have come. This is how we know it is the last hour.* [22]*Who is the liar? It is the man who denies that Jesus is the Christ. Such a man is the antichrist—he denies the Father and the Son.* (1 John 2:18, 22 NIV)

There are a number of pictures, or signs of the Beast, attached to the Antichrist. These pictures are the subject of literally thousands of prophetic speculations:

- The woman/Babylon—riding the Beast
- Seven heads
- Seven hills on which the woman sits
- Seven kings—Five have fallen, one is, the other is yet to come
- In Revelation 17 the Beast is identified as "an eighth king"
- 666—the number of the Beast
- The ten horns = ten kings who will serve along with the Beast

> ### A CLOSER LOOK
> #### Double Application of Prophecy
>
> Revelation is an example of the double application of prophecy, both to those to whom it was originally written and to the saints at a later time.
>
> Jesus' first coming had many examples of this double application of prophecy. Prophecies that were fulfilled in a partial way in Old Testament events found their ultimate and complete fulfillment in the life of Christ.
>
> The book of Revelation obviously points to the Roman Empire and the emperor Domitian in its pictures of the Beast. But it is also just as obvious that there is a greater fulfillment to be seen here—one that can come only at the end of time.
>
> Is it wrong to speculate about what these pictures might mean? No, as long as you never confuse speculation about God's Word with the perfect truth of God's Word. During Word War II many believers were absolutely certain that Hitler was the Antichrist. They turned out to be wrong. We must have the humility to recognize that we could be just as wrong about many of our speculations today.

2. A second beast/the _____

   In order to promote his program more efficiently, the Antichrist will have an important lieutenant. He is the "second beast" (Revelation 13:11–18), and his sole duty is to promote the purposes and expedite the worship of the first Beast, the Man of Sin.

3. The two _____

   Revelation 11 talks about two witnesses who will prophesy and picture the judgment of God, much like the great Old Testament prophets. They will be killed by the Beast in Jerusalem and will be resurrected by God into heaven as their enemies look on.

4. The 144,000

   12,000 sealed saints from each of the tribes of Israel (Revelation 7:4–8). They are pure believers in the midst of the tribulations of the last days (Revelation 14:1, 5).

Don't forget. All of these characters play only bit parts when compared to the leading character in this drama—Jesus Christ.

- Jesus will _____ the Beast and his lieutenant.

  And then the lawless one will be revealed, whom the Lord Jesus will overthrow with the breath of his mouth and destroy by the splendor of his coming. (2 Thessalonians 2:8 NIV)

- Jesus will redeem the two _____ .

  Then they heard a loud voice from heaven saying to them, "Come up here." And they went up to heaven in a cloud, while their enemies looked on. (Revelation 11:12 NIV)

- Jesus will lead the 144,000 to _____ .

  They follow the Lamb wherever he goes. They were purchased from among men and offered as firstfruits to God and the Lamb. (Revelation 14:4 NIV)

- Jesus will return in absolute _____ .

  For the Lord himself will come down from heaven with a mighty shout and with the soul-stirring cry of the archangel and the great trumpet-call of God. (1 Thessalonians 4:16 LB)

  [14b]Look, the Lord is coming with many thousands of his holy angels to [15]judge every person . . . (Jude 14b–15 NCV)

  Look, he is coming with the clouds, and every eye will see him . . . (Revelation 1:7 NIV)

  We wait for the blessed hope—the glorious appearing of our great God and Savior, Jesus Christ. (Titus 2:13 NIV)

Discovery Questions

1. Each picture Jesus uses to describe his second coming speaks of it being unexpected and soon. How do we reconcile this picture with the fact that it has been almost two thousand years since these words were written? What does the unexpected nature of Jesus' return reveal about how we need to live until that moment occurs?

2. As you heard about the cast of people associated with the events of the end times, what did you feel? Despair, fear, sadness, anger, hope, joy, victory, confusion, or something else? Explain what you felt and why.

3. How might your recognition of the truth that Jesus is coming at any moment have changed the way you faced one situation today? How could it change the way you face one situation tomorrow?

4. When you think about the immediate and unexpected nature of the promised second coming, what changes in your behavior toward others would you like to see as a result?

Did You Get It? How has this week's study helped you see that all of history's focus is on the person of Jesus Christ?

Share with Someone: Think of a person you can encourage with the truth you learned in this session. Write their name in the space below and pray for God to provide that opportunity this week.

LIVING ON PURPOSE
Evangelism

One of the most powerful aspects of the truth of the second coming of Jesus is its motivation to share our faith. Write down the name of one person for whose salvation you can pray.

Name: _____

Share the name with the group, and commit to pray together for those who do not yet know Jesus. Ask God to open doors of opportunity and be ready to talk to them about the hope and joy you have found in Christ.

PRAYER DIRECTION

Take a few minutes of prayer to personally express to Jesus your gratitude for his promised second coming.

3

SESSION THREE

EVENTS OF
THE END TIMES

CATCHING UP

1. Who did you share last week's truth with?

2. What did you learn during last week's "Living on Purpose" activity? As a result of your commitment to pray for the salvation of another, did you see God open any doors? Share what happened.

Key Verse

After that, we who are still alive and are left will be caught up together with them in the clouds to meet the Lord in the air. And so we will be with the Lord forever.

1 Thessalonians 4:17 (NIV)

BIBLE TEACHING
Watch the video lesson now and take notes in your outline on pages 23–28.

Events of the End Times

Jesus Christ is _____ to this earth again.

Just like he came the first time—in a visible, physical, bodily form—Jesus is coming to this earth again! Although Christians disagree about the order of events surrounding his return, of his actual return there can be no doubt. His second coming is spoken of even more clearly than his first coming.

> *⁹After he [Jesus] said this, he was taken up before their very eyes, and a cloud hid him from their sight. ¹⁰They were looking intently up into the sky as he was going, when suddenly two men dressed in white stood beside them. ¹¹"Men of Galilee," they said, "why do you stand here looking into the sky? This same Jesus, who has been taken from you into heaven, will come back in the same way you have seen him go into heaven."* (Acts 1:9–11 NIV)

> *²"There are many rooms in my Father's house; I would not tell you this if it were not true. I am going there to prepare a place for you. ³After I go and prepare a place for you, I will come back and take you to be with me so that you may be where I am."* (John 14:2–3 NCV)

There are four end-time events that every believer needs to understand: the tribulation, the rapture, the visible return of Christ, and the millennium.

The Tribulation

Revelation 4–18 describes the tribulation in detail. The signs that accompany Jesus' second coming (see page 6) were a description of many of the occurrences in this seven-year period. The time of tribulation includes the battle of Armageddon, the great final battle (Revelation 16:16).

Characteristics of the Tribulation:

- It will be _____, not localized.
- _____ will realize and act like the end is at hand.

The Rapture

A FRESH WORD

Rapture

The word "rapture" comes from the Latin translation of 1 Thessalonians 4:17. The original Greek word is translated "caught up" in English.

The rapture is when Jesus gathers all believers to be with him, giving each a resurrected, glorified body. This is to be distinguished from the visible return of Jesus in which all will see him and he will judge the nations and establish the kingdom. Many see the rapture as an event hidden to all but believers and occurring years before Jesus' visible return. Others see the rapture and Jesus' visible return as happening simultaneously.

Although there is some question about the exact time of the rapture, the questions we have about exactly *when* it will happen shouldn't detract from the assurance that it *will* happen.

First Thessalonians 4:13–18 gives the most detail about what will happen when the Lord raptures the church.

> *16For the Lord himself will come down from heaven, with a loud command, with the voice of the archangel and with the trumpet call of God, and the dead in Christ will rise first.*

¹⁷After that, we who are still alive and are left will be caught up together with them in the clouds to meet the Lord in the air. And so we will be with the Lord forever. ¹⁸Therefore encourage each other with these words. (1 Thessalonians 4:16–18 NIV)

1. The Lord _____ .

2. The dead in Christ will _____ .

   ⁴²So will it be with the resurrection of the dead. The body that is sown is perishable, it is raised imperishable; ⁴³it is sown in dishonor, it is raised in glory; it is sown in weakness, it is raised in power. (1 Corinthians 15:42–43 NIV)

3. We who are alive shall be _____ with them.

   . . . we who are still alive and are left will be caught up together with them . . . (1 Thessalonians 4:17 NIV)

4. We _____ the Lord in the air and we will be with the Lord forever.

The timing of the _____

Amillennial and postmillennial views regard the rapture of the church and the visible second coming of Christ as occurring one right after the other or at the same time.

The premillennial view sees an order. There are three general ideas as to what this order might be:

1. Pretribulation rapture—the rapture occurs right before the tribulation begins.

2. Midtribulation rapture—the rapture occurs 3½ years into the tribulation.

3. Posttribulation rapture—the rapture occurs at the end of the seven-year tribulation.

The Visible Return of Christ

The visible return of Christ is different from the rapture. At his return, all the earth will see Jesus returning, and he will establish his reign and rule on the earth.

> *"At that time the sign of the Son of Man will appear in the sky, and all the nations of the earth will mourn. They will see the Son of Man coming on the clouds of the sky, with power and great glory."* (Matthew 24:30 NIV)

The Millennium

The millennium is the term used to point to the thousand-year reign of Christ spoken of in Revelation 20:1–6.

> *[1]And I saw an angel coming down out of heaven, having the key to the Abyss and holding in his hand a great chain. [2]He seized the dragon, that ancient serpent, who is the devil, or Satan, and bound him for a thousand years. [3]He threw him into the Abyss, and locked and sealed it over him, to keep him from deceiving the nations anymore until the thousand years were ended. After that, he must be set free for a short time. [4]I saw thrones on which were seated those who had been given authority to judge. And I saw the souls of those who had been beheaded because of their testimony for Jesus and because of the word of God. They had not worshiped the beast or his image and had not received his mark on their foreheads or their hands. They came to life and reigned with Christ a thousand years. [5](The rest of the dead did not come to life until the thousand years were ended.) This is the first resurrection. [6]Blessed and holy are those who have part in the first resurrection. The second death has no power over them, but they will be priests of God and of Christ and will reign with him for a thousand years.* (Revelation 20:1–6 NIV)

Three major views of this thousand-year reign of Christ:

1. Postmillennial (Jesus comes again after the millennium)

   This view holds that the kingdom of God is now being extended in the world through the preaching of the gospel and the saving work of the Holy Spirit in the hearts of individuals. The world will eventually be Christianized, and the return of Christ will occur at the close of a long period of righteousness and peace commonly called the "millennium." This will not be a literal one thousand years, but actually an extended period of time.

   Strength: Optimistic view of the power of the gospel to change the world; hope for the fulfillment of the Great Commission.

   Weakness: Practically, this view is hard to reconcile with what's happening in the world. Biblically, it is hard to reconcile with the strong teaching of the final period of tribulation.

2. Amillennial (Jesus comes again without an earthly millennium)

   Until the end, there will be parallel development of both good and evil, God's kingdom and Satan's. After the second coming of Christ at the end of the world, there will be a general resurrection and general judgment of all people. The thousand-year reign of Christ is not literal; it is symbolic of Jesus' work on earth from his resurrection until his second coming.

   Strength: Answers questions about such things as resurrected saints living in an unregenerate world for a thousand years until the final judgment.

   Weakness: Must see a great deal of the second coming prophecies as spiritual symbols rather than actual events.

3. Premillennial (Jesus comes again before the millennium)

Premillennialism is the view that holds that the second coming of Christ will occur prior to the millennium and will establish Christ's kingdom on this earth for a literal one thousand years. The duration of Christ's kingdom will be one thousand years. Its location will be on this earth. Its government will be the personal presence of Christ reigning as King. And it will fulfill all the yet unfulfilled promises about Christ's earthly kingdom.

Strength: Attempts to seek understanding of all Scriptures relating to the second coming rather than ignoring those that are difficult to understand. A more literal view of Scripture.

Weakness: Is often marked by overcomplicated charts and with wrong guesses and differing opinions about the meaning of the symbols.

KEY PERSONAL PERSPECTIVE
Four Encouragements in These Four Events

1. The truth of the tribulation encourages me. Just because things get worse does not mean God will not soon make them better.

2. The truth of the rapture encourages me. God will take his children home.

3. The truth of Jesus' visible return encourages me. Jesus will ultimately be Lord of all.

4. The truth of the millennium encourages me. God has a plan that extends into eternity.

   What can be seen lasts only for a time, but what cannot be seen lasts forever. (2 Corinthians 4:18b GNT)

DISCOVERY QUESTIONS

1. How can the truth of the second coming become a unifying truth for all Christians, despite our possible disagreement regarding the order of events surrounding Christ's return?

2. What are you looking forward to when Jesus comes again? If you struggle with the idea of leaving this world behind, what specifically keeps you from longing for his return? What might help you overcome this obstacle and develop a passion for Jesus' visible return?

3. As he saw the tension in the faces of his followers the night before he went to the cross, Jesus gave them this tender promise:

> ²"In my Father's house are many rooms; if it were not so, I would have told you. I am going there to prepare a place for you. ³And if I go and prepare a place for you, I will come back and take you to be with me that you also may be where I am." (John 14:2–3 NIV)

As a follower of Jesus, how do his words here make you feel?

Did You Get It? How has this week's study helped you see the significance of the truths of Jesus' visible return, the tribulation, the rapture, and the millennium?

Share with Someone: Think of a person you can encourage with the truth you learned in this session. Write their name in the space below and pray for God to provide that opportunity this week.

LIVING ON PURPOSE
Fellowship

We all need encouragement, and there is no greater source than the hope we find in Christ. After teaching them the truth of the second coming, Paul wrote to the believers in Thessalonica:

> *Therefore encourage each other with these words.* (1 Thessalonians 4:18 NIV)

Who do you know who needs the hope of Christ today? Take some time before your next meeting to write them a brief note of encouragement, and be sure to include in your note the eternal hope we have because of Jesus' love.

PRAYER DIRECTION

Take some time as a group to talk about your specific prayer requests and to pray for one another. Thank God for the hope he has given you through the life, death, and resurrection of Jesus Christ.

Session four

4

PREPARING FOR
THE END TIMES

CATCHING UP

Who did you share last week's truth with? Were you able to encourage someone with the hope of Christ's return? Briefly share your experience as a witness to the hope Christ gives us.

Key Verse

You too, be patient and stand firm, because the Lord's coming is near.

James 5:8 (NIV)

BIBLE TEACHING
Watch the video lesson now and take notes in your outline on pages 33–36.

What Happens at the End of Time?

*For believers—*_____*!*

> *So Christ was sacrificed once to take away the sins of many people; and he will appear a second time, not to bear sin, but to bring salvation to those who are waiting for him.* (Hebrews 9:28 NIV)

> *And when the head Shepherd comes, your reward will be a never-ending share in his glory and honor.* (1 Peter 5:4 NLT)

> *Dear friends, now we are children of God, and we have not yet been shown what we will be in the future. But we know that when Christ comes again, we will be like him, because we will see him as he really is.* (1 John 3:2 NCV)

The riches that we receive from Jesus—salvation, worshiping him in a perfect eternity, and crowns of glory—come to us based solely on God's grace. But we will not just receive Jesus' riches, we will become more like Jesus in all of eternity. What an incredible reward we have to look forward to!

For the Jewish people—_____.

> *[11]Again I ask: Did they stumble so as to fall beyond recovery? Not at all! Rather, because of their transgression, salvation has come to the Gentiles to make Israel envious. [12]But if their transgression means riches for the world, and their loss means riches for the Gentiles, how much greater riches will their fullness bring!....[25]I do not want you to be ignorant of this mystery, brothers, so that you may not be conceited: Israel has experienced a hardening in part until the full number of the Gentiles has come in. [26]And so all Israel will be saved, as it is written: "The deliverer will come from Zion; he will turn godlessness away from Jacob."* (Romans 11:11-12, 25-26 NIV)

There are two views of this passage:

1. The literal nation of Israel has to be restored under the rule of a King David.

2. There will be a great revival among the Jewish people at the end of time.

Whichever way you see these verses, they clearly tell us that, before the end, many Jewish people will be brought to faith in Christ.

For unbelievers—_____.

> *[11]Then I saw a great white throne and him who was seated on it. Earth and sky fled from his presence, and there was no place for them. [12]And I saw the dead, great and small, standing before the throne, and books were opened. Another book was opened, which is the book of life. The dead were judged according to what they had done as recorded in the books....[15]If anyone's name was not found written in the book of life, he was thrown into the lake of fire.*
> (Revelation 20:11-12, 15 NIV)

If we do not trust Christ in this life, all that we have to stand on when we come before God is what we've done, and it's not enough.

What Should Our Attitude Be?

1. Be alert and _____ .

> *"Be on guard! Be alert! You do not know when that time will come."* (Mark 13:33 NIV)

> *"If he comes suddenly, do not let him find you sleeping."* (Mark 13:36 NIV)

The truth of the approaching light of his coming should wake us up to the real and crying needs that are all around us.

2. Be alert and _____ .

> *So then, let us not be like others, who are asleep, but let us be alert and self-controlled.* (1 Thessalonians 5:6 NIV)

> *Therefore, prepare your minds for action; be self-controlled; set your hope fully on the grace to be given you when Jesus Christ is revealed.* (1 Peter 1:13 NIV)

> *The end of all things is near. Therefore be clear minded and self-controlled so that you can pray.* (1 Peter 4:7 NIV)

How does the truth of the second coming make us more self-controlled? By helping us to keep the truth in perspective and see things as they really are, not letting anything distract us from the priorities that really matter as we expectantly wait for Christ's return.

3. Live _____ lives.

> [11]*Since everything will be destroyed in this way, what kind of people ought you to be? You ought to live holy and godly lives* [12a]*as you look forward to the day of God and speed its coming.* (2 Peter 3:11–12a NIV)

If you think that no one cares about your character, that it goes unnoticed, you're wrong. The way that you witness for Christ in some way impacts God's timetable for his return.

4. Be _____ and _____ wait.

> *You too, be patient and stand firm, because the Lord's coming is near.* (James 5:8 NIV)

> *Therefore you do not lack any spiritual gift as you eagerly wait for our Lord Jesus Christ to be revealed.* (1 Corinthians 1:7 NIV)

Anticipation is the attitude of being patient and eager at the same time. Why wait until Jesus comes again to begin enjoying it? We can enjoy his coming right now by anticipating it in our hearts.

5. Long for his _____ .

> *Now there is in store for me the crown of righteousness, which the Lord, the righteous Judge, will award to me on that day—and not only to me, but also to all who have longed for his appearing.* (2 Timothy 4:8 NIV)

> [11]*For the grace of God that brings salvation has appeared to all men.* [12]*It teaches us to say "No" to ungodliness and worldly passions, and to live self-controlled, upright and godly lives in this present age,* [13]*while we wait for the blessed hope—the glorious appearing of our great God and Savior, Jesus Christ.* (Titus 2:11–13 NIV)

Don't let the circumstances of your daily life keep you from looking to the blessed hope that is in your future.

How can the truth of Jesus' second coming make a real difference in your life and help you hold on to that hope? Like the Apostle John, let the knowledge of what God is going to do draw your heart out in worship.

DISCOVERY QUESTIONS

1. According to Hebrews 9:28 and 1 Peter 5:4, what reward is promised to believers when Christ returns? Does the promise of this reward influence your outlook on the return of Jesus? Why or why not? Does the fact you'll be rewarded cause you any feelings of guilt? Why or why not?

2. Talk together about your personal experience with the daily attitudes God encourages us to have toward the second coming.

   Be alert and watchful. What helps you think about the fact that Jesus is going to come again?

   Be alert and self-controlled. How does the truth of Christ's visible return help you say "no" to temptation and "yes" to spiritual disciplines such as prayer and serving others?

Live holy lives. What helps you to live motivated less by fear and more by a desire to please God?

Be patient and eagerly wait. What lessons have you learned (or seen in others) that help you remember not to hurry God?

Long for his return! What are you looking forward to when Jesus comes again?

If you do not know Jesus personally and you are not sure that your name is written in the Book of Life, please don't miss this opportunity to talk about this with a friend in the group or with your group host.

> ## "HOW TO BECOME A FOLLOWER OF JESUS CHRIST"
>
> Have you ever surrendered your life to Jesus Christ? Take a few minutes with your group to watch a brief video by Pastor Rick Warren on how to become part of the family of God. It is included on the Main Menu of this DVD.

Did You Get It? How has this week's study helped you to see that the second coming is a real event, with eternal consequences for every person on earth?

Share with Someone: Think of a person you can encourage with the truth you learned in this session. Write their name in the space below and pray for God to provide that opportunity this week.

LIVING ON PURPOSE AND PRAYER DIRECTION
Worship

(This week, combine your prayer time and purpose activity by worshiping God together.)

In the last chapter of the book of Revelation, John wrote:

> [8]*I, John, am the one who heard and saw these things. And when I had heard and seen them, I fell down to worship at the feet of the angel who had been showing them to me.* [9]*But he said to me, "Do not do it! I am a fellow servant with you and with your brothers the prophets and of all who keep the words of this book. Worship God!"* (Revelation 22:8-9 NIV)

There is no better summation of our study of the end times than those two powerful words of invitation, "Worship God!" Hope is realizing that God will have the last word. As a group, pray through the following verses, praising God for who he is. Have someone read the verse, and then several of you thank God for the truths in that verse. Do the same with each verse, as time allows.

> *When I saw him, I fell at his feet as though dead. Then he placed his right hand on me and said: "Do not be afraid. I am the First and the Last."* (Revelation 1:17 NIV)

> *Each of the four living creatures had six wings and was covered with eyes all around, even under his wings. Day and night they never stop saying: "Holy, holy, holy is the Lord God Almighty, who was, and is, and is to come."* (Revelation 4:8 NIV)

> [10b]*They lay their crowns before the throne and say:* [11]*"You are worthy, our Lord and God, to receive glory and honor and power, for you created all things, and by your will they were created and have their being."* (Revelation 4:10b-11 NIV)

> [11]*Then I looked again, and I heard the singing of thousands and millions of angels around the throne and the living beings and the elders.* [12]*And they sang in a mighty chorus: "The Lamb is worthy—the Lamb who was killed. He is worthy to receive power and riches and wisdom and strength and honor and glory and blessing."* (Revelation 5:11-12 NLT)

> [3]*I heard a loud shout from the throne, saying, "Look, the home of God is now among his people! He will live with them, and they will be his people. God himself will be with them.* [4]*He will remove all of their sorrows, and there will be no more death or sorrow or crying or pain. For the old world and its evils are gone forever."* [5a]*And the one sitting on the throne said, "Look, I am making all things new!"* (Revelation 21:3-5a NLT)

Small Group Resources

HELPS FOR HOSTS

Top Ten Ideas for New Hosts

Congratulations! As the host of your small group, you have responded to the call to help shepherd Jesus' flock. Few other tasks in the family of God surpass the contribution you will be making.

As you prepare to facilitate your group, whether it is one session or the entire series, here are a few thoughts to keep in mind. We encourage you to read and review these tips with each new discussion host before he or she leads.

Remember you are not alone. God knows everything about you, and he knew you would be asked to facilitate your group. Even though you may not feel ready, this is common for all good hosts. God promises, *"I will never leave you; I will never abandon you"* (Hebrews 13:5 TEV). Whether you are facilitating for one evening, several weeks, or a lifetime, you will be blessed as you serve.

1. **Don't try to do it alone.** Pray right now for God to help you build a healthy team. If you can enlist a cohost to help you shepherd the group, you will find your experience much richer. This is your chance to involve as many people as you can in building a healthy group. All you have to do is ask people to help. You'll be surprised at the response.

2. **Be friendly and be yourself.** God wants to use your unique gifts and temperament. Be sure to greet people at the door with a big smile . . . this can set the mood for the whole gathering. Remember, they are taking as big a step to show up at your house as you are to lead this group! Don't try to do things exactly like another host; do them in a way that fits you. Admit when you don't have an answer and apologize when you make a mistake. Your group will love you for it and you'll sleep better at night.

3. **Prepare for your meeting ahead of time.** Review the session and write down your responses to each question. Pay special attention to exercises that ask group members to do something other than engage in discussion. These exercises will help your group live what the Bible teaches, not just talk about it. Be sure you understand how an exercise works. If the exercise employs one of the items in the Small Group Resources section (such as the Group Guidelines), be sure to look over that item so you'll know how it works.

4. **Pray for your group members by name.** Before you begin your session, take a few moments and pray for each member by name. You may want to review the prayer list at least once a week. Ask God to use your time together to touch the heart of every person in your group. Expect God to lead you to whomever he wants you to encourage or challenge in a special way. If you listen, God will surely lead.

5. **When you ask a question, be patient.** Someone will eventually respond. Sometimes people need a moment or two of silence to think about the question. If silence doesn't bother you, it won't bother anyone else. After someone responds, affirm the response with a simple "thanks" or "great answer." Then ask, "How about somebody else?" or "Would someone who hasn't shared like to add anything?" Be sensitive to new people or reluctant members who aren't ready to say, pray, or do anything. If you give them a safe setting, they will blossom over time. If someone in your group is a "wallflower" who sits silently through every session, consider talking to them privately and encouraging them to participate. Let them know how important they are to you—that they are loved and appreciated—and that the group would value their input. Remember, still water often runs deep.

6. **Provide transitions between questions.** Ask if anyone would like to read the paragraph or Bible passage. Don't call on anyone, but ask for a volunteer, and then be patient until someone begins. Be sure to thank the person who reads aloud.

7. **Break into smaller groups occasionally.** With a greater opportunity to talk in a small circle, people will connect more with the study, apply more quickly what they're learning, and ultimately get more out of their small group experience. A small circle also encourages a quiet person to participate and tends to minimize the effects of a more vocal or dominant member.

8. **Small circles are also helpful during prayer time.** People who are unaccustomed to praying aloud will feel more comfortable trying it with just two or three others. Also, prayer requests won't take as much time, so circles will have more time to actually pray. When you gather back with the whole group, you can have one person from each circle briefly update everyone on the prayer requests from their subgroups. The other great aspect of subgrouping is that it fosters leadership development. As you ask people in the group to facilitate discussion or to lead a prayer circle, it gives them a small leadership step that can build their confidence.

9. **Rotate facilitators occasionally.** You may be perfectly capable of hosting each time, but you will help others grow in their faith and gifts if you give them opportunities to host the group.

10. **One final challenge (for new or first-time hosts).** Before your first opportunity to lead, look up each of the six passages that follow. Read each one as a devotional exercise to help prepare you with a shepherd's heart. Trust us on this one. If you do this, you will be more than ready for your first meeting.

Matthew 9:36–38 (NIV)
[36]When Jesus saw the crowds, he had compassion on them, because they were harassed and helpless, like sheep without a shepherd. [37]Then he said to his disciples, "The harvest is plentiful but the workers are few. [38]Ask the Lord of the harvest, therefore, to send out workers into his harvest field."

John 10:14–15 (NIV)
[14]I am the good shepherd; I know my sheep and my sheep know me—[15]just as the Father knows me and I know the Father—and I lay down my life for the sheep.

1 Peter 5:2–4 (NIV)

²Be shepherds of God's flock that is under your care, serving as overseers—not because you must, but because you are willing, as God wants you to be; ³not greedy for money, but eager to serve; not lording it over those entrusted to you, but being examples to the flock. ⁴And when the Chief Shepherd appears, you will receive the crown of glory that will never fade away.

Philippians 2:1–5 (NIV)

¹If you have any encouragement from being united with Christ, if any comfort from his love, if any fellowship with the Spirit, if any tenderness and compassion, ²then make my joy complete by being like-minded, having the same love, being one in spirit and purpose. ³Do nothing out of selfish ambition or vain conceit, but in humility consider others better than yourselves. ⁴Each of you should look not only to your own interests, but also to the interests of others. ⁵Your attitude should be the same as that of Jesus Christ.

Hebrews 10:23–25 (NIV)

²³Let us hold unswervingly to the hope we profess, for he who promised is faithful. ²⁴And let us consider how we may spur one another on toward love and good deeds. ²⁵Let us not give up meeting together, as some are in the habit of doing, but let us encourage one another—and all the more as you see the Day approaching.

1 Thessalonians 2:7–8, 11–12 (NIV)

⁷. . . but we were gentle among you, like a mother caring for her little children. ⁸We loved you so much that we were delighted to share with you not only the gospel of God but our lives as well, because you had become so dear to us. . . . ¹¹For you know that we dealt with each of you as a father deals with his own children, ¹²encouraging, comforting and urging you to live lives worthy of God, who calls you into his kingdom and glory.

FREQUENTLY ASKED QUESTIONS

How long will this group meet?

This volume of *Foundations: The Second Coming* is four sessions long. We encourage your group to add a fifth session for a celebration. In your final session, each group member may decide if he or she desires to continue on for another study. At that time you may also want to do some informal evaluation, discuss your Group Guidelines, and decide which study you want to do next. We recommend you visit our website at **www.saddlebackresources.com** for more video-based small group studies.

Who is the host?

The host is the person who coordinates and facilitates your group meetings. In addition to a host, we encourage you to select one or more group members to lead your group discussions. Several other responsibilities can be rotated, including refreshments, prayer requests, worship, or keeping up with those who miss a meeting. Shared ownership in the group helps everybody grow.

Where do we find new group members?

Recruiting new members can be a challenge for groups, especially new groups with just a few people, or existing groups that lose a few people along the way. We encourage you to use the *Circles of Life* diagram on page 50 of this DVD study guide to brainstorm a list of people from your workplace, church, school, neighborhood, family, and so on. Then pray for the people on each member's list. Allow each member to invite several people from their list. Some groups fear that newcomers will interrupt the intimacy that members have built over time. However, groups that welcome newcomers generally gain strength with the infusion of new blood. Remember, the next person you add just might become a friend for eternity. Logistically, groups find different ways to add members. Some groups remain permanently open, while others choose to open periodically, such as at the beginning or end of a study. If your group becomes too large for easy, face-to-face conversations, you can subgroup, forming a second discussion group in another room.

How do we handle the child care needs in our group?

Child care needs must be handled very carefully. This is a sensitive issue. We suggest you seek creative solutions as a group. One common solution is to have the adults meet in the living room and share the cost of a babysitter (or two) who can be with the kids in another part of the house. Another popular option is to have one home for the kids and a second home (close by) for the adults. If desired, the adults could rotate the responsibility of providing a lesson for the kids. This last option is great with school-age kids and can be a huge blessing to families.

GROUP GUIDELINES

It's a good idea for every group to put words to their shared values, expectations, and commitments. Such guidelines will help you avoid unspoken agendas and unmet expectations. We recommend you discuss your guidelines during Session One in order to lay the foundation for a healthy group experience. Feel free to modify anything that does not work for your group.

We agree to the following values:

Clear Purpose	To grow healthy spiritual lives by building a healthy small group community
Group Attendance	To give priority to the group meeting (call if I am absent or late)
Safe Environment	To create a safe place where people can be heard and feel loved (no quick answers, snap judgments, or simple fixes)
Be Confidential	To keep anything that is shared strictly confidential and within the group
Conflict Resolution	To avoid gossip and to immediately resolve any concerns by following the principles of Matthew 18:15–17
Spiritual Health	To give group members permission to speak into my life and help me live a healthy, balanced spiritual life that is pleasing to God
Limit Our Freedom	To limit our freedom by not serving or consuming alcohol during small group meetings or events so as to avoid causing a weaker brother or sister to stumble (1 Corinthians 8:1–13; Romans 14:19–21)

Welcome Newcomers   To invite friends who might benefit from this study and warmly welcome newcomers

Building Relationships To get to know the other members of the group and pray for them regularly

Other   _____

We have also discussed and agreed on the following items:

Child Care

_____

_____

Starting Time

_____

Ending Time

_____

If you haven't already done so, take a few minutes to fill out the *Small Group Calendar* on page 54.

CIRCLES OF LIFE—SMALL GROUP CONNECTIONS

Discover who you can connect in community

Use this chart to help carry out one of the values in the Group Guidelines, to "Welcome Newcomers."

"Follow me, and I will make you fishers of men." (Matthew 4:19 KJV)

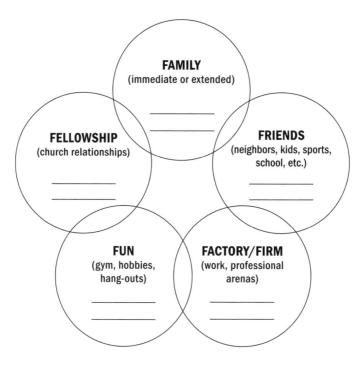

Follow this simple three-step process:

1. List 1–2 people in each circle.

2. Prayerfully select one person or couple from your list and tell your group about them.

3. Give them a call and invite them to your next meeting. Over 50 percent of those invited to a small group say, "Yes!"

SMALL GROUP PRAYER AND PRAISE REPORT

This is a place where you can write each other's requests for prayer. You can also make a note when God answers a prayer. Pray for each other's requests. If you're new to group prayer, it's okay to pray silently or to pray by using just one sentence: "God, please help

_____ to _____ . "

DATE	PERSON	PRAYER REQUEST	PRAISE REPORT

SMALL GROUP PRAYER AND PRAISE REPORT

DATE	PERSON	PRAYER REQUEST	PRAISE REPORT

SMALL GROUP PRAYER AND PRAISE REPORT

DATE	PERSON	PRAYER REQUEST	PRAISE REPORT

SMALL GROUP CALENDAR

Healthy groups share responsibilities and group ownership. It might take some time for this to develop. Shared ownership ensures that responsibility for the group doesn't fall to one person. Use the calendar to keep track of social events, mission projects, birthdays, or days off. Complete this calendar at your first or second meeting. Planning ahead will increase attendance and shared ownership.

DATE	LESSON	LOCATION	FACILITATOR	SNACK OR MEAL
5/4	Session 2	Chris and Andrea	Jim Brown	Phil and Karen

ANSWER KEY

Session One:
Signs of Jesus' Coming

First Warning: Don't lose personal <u>responsibility</u> in the midst of historical and theological <u>curiosity</u>.

2. What is the underlying timeless principle? In a word, <u>hope</u>.

Second Warning: Don't lose the <u>delight</u> in the <u>details</u>.

Third Warning: Watch out for <u>polarization</u> in teaching about the second coming.

- False <u>christs</u>
- <u>Wars</u>
- <u>Earthquakes</u>
- <u>Famine</u>

Jesus' warning about these signs: don't be <u>deceived</u>!

- <u>Apostasy</u>
- <u>Increase</u> of personal evil
- <u>Scoffers</u> will come
- Many <u>false</u> prophets

Session Two:
God's Timing

- Like a <u>bridegroom</u>
- Like the destruction of <u>Sodom</u>
- Like <u>Noah's flood</u>
- Like a <u>thief</u> in the night

- The time of Jesus' return is <u>soon</u>.
- The time of Jesus' return is known only by <u>God</u>.
- The time of Jesus' return is <u>unexpected</u>.

1. The Man of Lawlessness/the Beast/ the <u>Antichrist</u>
2. A second beast/the <u>False Prophet</u>
3. The two <u>witnesses</u>

- Jesus will <u>destroy</u> the Beast and his lieutenant.
- Jesus will redeem the two <u>witnesses</u>.
- Jesus will lead the 144,000 to <u>victory</u>.
- Jesus will return in absolute <u>glory</u>.

Session Three:
Events of the End Times

Jesus Christ is <u>coming</u> to this earth again

- It will be <u>worldwide</u>, not localized.
- <u>All</u> will realize and act like the end is at hand.

1. The Lord <u>descends</u>.
2. The dead in Christ will <u>rise</u>.
3. We who are alive shall be <u>caught up</u> with them.
4. We <u>meet</u> the Lord in the air and we will be with the Lord forever.

The timing of the <u>rapture</u>

Session Four:
Preparing for the End Times

For believers—<u>Reward!</u>

For the Jewish people—<u>Restoration</u>.

For unbelievers—<u>Judgment</u>.

1. Be alert and <u>watchful</u>.
2. Be alert and <u>self-controlled</u>.
3. Live <u>holy</u> lives.
4. Be <u>patient</u> and <u>eagerly</u> wait.
5. Long for his <u>return</u>.

NOTES

KEY VERSES

One of the most effective ways to drive deeply into our lives the principles we are learning in this series is to memorize key Scriptures. For many, memorization is a new concept or one that has been difficult in the past. We encourage you to stretch yourself and try to memorize these four key verses. If possible, memorize these as a group and make them part of your group time. You may cut these apart and carry them in your wallet.

I have hidden your word in my heart that I might not sin against you.

Psalm 119:11 (NIV)

Session One

Therefore, prepare your minds for action; be self-controlled; set your hope fully on the grace to be given you when Jesus Christ is revealed.

1 Peter 1:13 (NIV)

Session Two

For you know very well that the day of the Lord will come like a thief in the night.

1 Thessalonians 5:2 (NIV)

Session Three

After that, we who are still alive and are left will be caught up together with them in the clouds to meet the Lord in the air. And so we will be with the Lord forever.

1 Thessalonians 4:17 (NIV)

Session Four

You too, be patient and stand firm, because the Lord's coming is near.

James 5:8 (NIV)

NOTES

We value your thoughts about what you've just read.
Please share them with us. You'll find contact information
in the back of this book.

The Purpose Driven® Life
A six-session video-based study for groups or individuals

Embark on a journey of discovery with this video-based study taught by Rick Warren. In it you will discover the answer to life's most fundamental question: "What on earth am I here for?"

And here's a clue to the answer: "It's not about you . . . You were created by God and for God, and until you understand that, life will never make sense. It is only in God that we discover our origin, our identity, our meaning, our purpose, our significance, and our destiny."

Whether you experience this adventure with a small group or on your own, this six-session, video-based study will change your life.

DVD Study Guide: 978-0-310-27866-5
DVD: 978-0-310-27864-1

Be sure to combine this study with your reading of the best-selling book, *The Purpose Driven® Life,* to give you or your small group the opportunity to discuss the implications and applications of living the life God created you to live.

Hardcover, Jacketed: 978-0-310-20571-5
Softcover: 978-0-310-27699-9

Pick up a copy today at your favorite bookstore!

Foundations: 11 Core Truths to Build Your Life On

Taught by Tom Holladay and Kay Warren

Foundations is a series of 11 four-week video studies covering the most important, foundational doctrines of the Christian faith. Study topics include:

The Bible—This study focuses on where the Bible came from, why it can be trusted, and how it can change your life.

DVD Study Guide: 978-0-310-27670-8
DVD: 978-0-310-27669-2

God—This study focuses not just on facts about God, but on how to know God himself in a more powerful and personal way.

DVD Study Guide: 978-0-310-27672-2
DVD: 978-0-310-27671-5

Jesus—As we look at what the Bible says about the person of Christ, we do so as people who are developing a lifelong relationship with Jesus.

DVD Study Guide: 978-0-310-27674-6
DVD: 978-0-310-27673-9

The Holy Spirit—This study focuses on the person, the presence, and the power of the Holy Spirit, and how you can be filled with the Holy Spirit on a daily basis.

DVD Study Guide: 978-0-310-27676-0
DVD: 978-0-310-27675-3

Creation—Each of us was personally created by a loving God. This study does not shy away from the great scientific and theological arguments that surround the creation/evolution debate. However, you will find the goal of this study is deepening your awareness of God as your Creator.

DVD Study Guide: 978-0-310-27678-4
DVD: 978-0-310-27677-7

Pick up a copy today at your favorite bookstore!

Salvation—This study focuses on God's solution to man's need for salvation, what Jesus Christ did for us on the cross, and the assurance and security of God's love and provision for eternity.

DVD Study Guide: 978-0-310-27682-1
DVD: 978-0-310-27679-1

Sanctification—This study focuses on the two natures of the Christian. We'll see the difference between grace and law, and how these two things work in our lives.

DVD Study Guide: 978-0-310-27684-5
DVD: 978-0-310-27683-8

Good and Evil—Why do bad things happen to good people? Through this study we'll see how and why God continues to allow evil to exist. The ultimate goal is to build up our faith and relationship with God as we wrestle with these difficult questions.

DVD Study Guide: 978-0-310-27687-6
DVD: 978-0-310-27686-9

The Afterlife—The Bible does not answer all the questions we have about what happens to us after we die; however, this study deals with what the Bible does tell us. This important study gives us hope and helps us move from a focus on the here and now to a focus on eternity.

DVD Study Guide: 978-0-310-27689-0
DVD: 978-0-310-27688-3

The Church—This study focuses on the birth of the church, the nature of the church, and the mission of the church.

DVD Study Guide: 978-0-310-27692-0
DVD: 978-0-310-27691-3

The Second Coming—This study addresses both the hope and the uncertainties surrounding the second coming of Jesus Christ.

DVD Study Guide: 978-0-310-27695-1
DVD: 978-0-310-27693-7

Pick up a copy today at your favorite bookstore!

Celebrate Recovery, Updated Curriculum Kit

This kit will provide your church with the tools necessary to start a successful Celebrate Recovery program. *Kit includes:*

- Introductory Guide for Leaders DVD
- Leader's Guide
- 4 Participant's Guides (one of each guide)
- CD-ROM with 25 lessons
- CD-ROM with sermon transcripts
- 4-volume audio CD sermon series

Curriculum Kit: 978-0-310-26847-5

Participant's Guide 4-pack

The Celebrate Recovery Participant's Guide 4-pack is a convenient resource when you're just getting started or if you need replacement guides for your program.

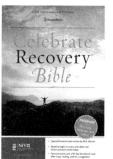

Celebrate Recovery Bible

With features based on eight principles Jesus voiced in his Sermon on the Mount, the new *Celebrate Recovery Bible* offers hope, encouragement, and empowerment for those struggling with the circumstances of their lives and the habits they are trying to control.

Hardcover: 978-0-310-92849-2
Softcover: 978-0-310-93810-1

Pick up a copy today at your favorite bookstore!

ZONDERVAN®
.com

Stepping Out of Denial into God's Grace

Participant's Guide 1 introduces the eight principles of recovery based on Jesus' words in the Beatitudes, and focuses on principles 1–3. Participants learn about denial, hope, sanity, and more.

Getting Right with God, Yourself, and Others

Participant's Guide 3 covers principles 5–7 based on Jesus' words in the Beatitudes. With courage and support from their fellow participants, people seeking recovery will find victory, forgiveness, and grace.

Taking an Honest and Spiritual Inventory

Participant's Guide 2 focuses on the fourth principle based on Jesus' words in the Beatitudes and builds on the Scripture, *"Happy are the pure in heart."* (Matthew 5:8) The participant will learn an invaluable principle for recovery and also take an in-depth spiritual inventory.

Growing in Christ While Helping Others

Participant's Guide 4 walks through the final steps of the eight recovery principles based on Jesus' words in the Beatitudes. In this final phase, participants learn to move forward in newfound freedom in Christ, learning how to give back to others. There's even a practical lesson called "Seven reasons we get stuck in our recoveries."

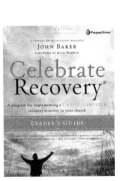

Leader's Guide

The Celebrate Recovery Leader's Guide gives you everything you need to facilitate your preparation time. Virtually walking you through every meeting, the Leader's Guide is a must-have for every leader on your Celebrate Recovery ministry team.

Pick up a copy today at your favorite bookstore!

ZONDERVAN®
.com

Wide Angle:
Framing Your Worldview

Christianity is much more than a religion. It is a worldview—a way of seeing all of life and the world around you. Your worldview impacts virtually every decision you make in life: moral decisions, relational decisions, financial decisions— everything. How you see the world determines how you face the world.

In this brand new study, Rick Warren and Chuck Colson discuss such key issues as moral relativism, tolerance, terrorism, creationism vs. Darwinism, sin and suffering. They explore in depth the Christian worldview as it relates to the most important questions in life:

- Why does it matter what I believe?

- How do I know what's true?

- Where do I come from?

- Why is the world so messed up?

- Is there a solution?

- What is my purpose in life?

Rick Warren   *Chuck Colson*

This study is as deep as it is wide, addressing vitally important topics for every follower of Christ.

DVD Study Guide: 978-1-4228-0083-6
DVD: 978-1-4228-0082-9

The Way of a Worshiper

The pursuit of God is the chase of a lifetime—in fact, it's been going on since the day you were born. The question is: Have you been the hunter or the prey?

This small group study is not about music. It's not even about going to church. It's about living your life as an offering of worship to God. It's about tapping into the source of power to live the Christian life. And it's about discovering the secret to friendship with God.

In these four video sessions, Buddy Owens helps you unpack the meaning of worship. Through his very practical, engaging, and at times surprising insights, Buddy shares truths from Scripture and from life that will help you understand in a new and deeper way just what it means to be a worshiper.

God is looking for worshipers. His invitation to friendship is open and genuine. Will you take him up on his offer? Will you give yourself to him in worship? Then come walk *The Way of a Worshiper* and discover the secret to friendship with God.

DVD Study Guide: 978-1-4228-0096-6
DVD: 978-1-4228-0095-9

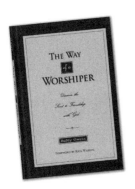

THE WAY of a WORSHIPER

Your study of this material will be greatly enhanced by reading the book, *The Way of a Worshiper: Discover the Secret to Friendship with God.*

Managing Our Finances God's Way

Did you know that there are over 2,350 verses in the Bible about money? Did you know that nearly half of Jesus' parables are about possessions? The Bible is packed with wise counsel about your financial life. In fact, Jesus had more to say about money than about heaven and hell combined.

Introducing a new video-based small group study that will inspire you to live debt free! Created by Saddleback Church and Crown Financial Ministries, learn what the Bible has to say about our finances from Rick Warren, Chip Ingram, Ron Blue, Howard Dayton, and Chuck Bentley as they address important topics like:

- God's Solution to Debt
- Saving and Investing
- Plan Your Spending
- Giving as an Act of Worship
- Enjoy What God Has Given You

Study includes:

- DVD with seven 20-minute lessons

- Workbook with seven lessons

- Resource CD with digital version of all worksheets that perform calculations automatically

- Contact information for help with answering questions

- Resources for keeping financial plans on track and making them lifelong habits

> **NOTE:** PARTICIPANTS DO NOT SHARE PERSONAL FINANCIAL INFORMATION WITH EACH OTHER.

DVD Study Guide: 978-1-4228-0083-6
DVD: 978-1-4228-0082-9

Share Your Thoughts

With the Author: Your comments will be forwarded to the author when you send them to *zauthor@zondervan.com*.

With Zondervan: Submit your review of this book by writing to *zreview@zondervan.com*.

Free Online Resources at

www.zondervan.com/hello

 Zondervan AuthorTracker: Be notified whenever your favorite authors publish new books, go on tour, or post an update about what's happening in their lives.

 Daily Bible Verses and Devotions: Enrich your life with daily Bible verses or devotions that help you start every morning focused on God.

 Free Email Publications: Sign up for newsletters on fiction, Christian living, church ministry, parenting, and more.

 Zondervan Bible Search: Find and compare Bible passages in a variety of translations at www.zondervanbiblesearch.com.

 Other Benefits: Register yourself to receive online benefits like coupons and special offers, or to participate in research.